T2·BQX·846

D0764547

J975.5
Cocke, William, 1960-
A historical album of
Virginia /
c1995.

Discarded by
Santa Maria Library

GAYLORD MG

A HISTORICAL ALBUM OF
VIRGINIA

A HISTORICAL ALBUM OF
VIRGINIA

William Cocke

THE MILLBROOK PRESS, Brookfield, Connecticut

Front and back cover: "View of Lexington, Va. The Military Institute and Washington College."
Painting by Casimir Bohn, 1856. Washington and Lee University, Lexington, Va.

Title page: Natural Bridge. Courtesy of the Virginia Division of Tourism.

Library of Congress Cataloging-in-Publication Data

Cocke, William, 1960-
    A historical album of Virginia / William Cocke.
        p. cm. — (Historical albums)
    Includes index.
    Summary: A history of Virginia, from its early exploration and
settlement to the state today.
    ISBN 1-56294-596-3 (lib. bdg.) ISBN 1-56294-856-3 (pbk.)
    1. Virginia—History—Juvenile literature. 2. Virginia—
Gazetteers—Juvenile literature. I. Title. II. Series.
F226.3.C63 1995
975.5—dc20   95-11775
                                                   CIP
                                                   AC

Created in association with Media Projects Incorporated

    C. Carter Smith, *Executive Editor*
    Kimberly Horstman, *Project Editor*
    William Cocke, *Principal Writer*
    Bernard Schleifer, *Art Director*
    John W. Kern, *Production Editor*
    Arlene Goldberg, *Cartographer*

Consultant: Nancy Andersen, Classroom Teacher,
Cub Run Elementary School, Centreville, Virginia,
Fairfax County Public Schools

Copyright © 1995 by The Millbrook Press, Inc.

All rights reserved, including the right of reproduction in whole or in part in any form.

Manufactured in the United States of America

10 9 8 7 6 5 4 3 2 1

CONTENTS

Introduction

Europeans first settled in Virginia more than 160 years before the United States was founded. Learning Virginia's history is, in many ways, the key to understanding the early history of the country.

Virginia is shaped roughly like a triangle. Its geography can be divided into three major regions: the coastal plain, also known as the Tidewater; the Piedmont, which extends to the foot of the Blue Ridge Mountains; and the Ridge and Valley Region. While the coastal region has always led the way in settlement and industry, the mountains in the western part of the state give Virginia its legendary beauty.

Virginia and its people were involved in many prominent events that shaped our national history. The English established their first New World colony at Jamestown early in the 17th century. After years of hardship, the colony prospered and grew, enticing thousands of people to make the journey across the ocean and settle in America. By the 1760s, Virginia leaders played a crucial role in the revolution and in the first decades of American independence, including offering the nation twenty-four years of Virginia-born presidents.

During the Civil War, the state became the main battleground between North and South and produced some of the most famous and talented leaders of that conflict, including Robert E. Lee and Thomas "Stonewall" Jackson. By World War II, the Norfolk-Hampton Roads area was one of the country's major shipbuilding centers. In the 1970s and 1980s, Virginia's strong connection to national affairs continued, with the federal government being the largest employer in the state.

Today, Virginians live with the reminders of their distinguished history all around them. Despite being one of the oldest settled regions in America, Virginia still retains much of its charm and rural character. Virginians remain proud of their past, yet they are looking ahead to the future.

THE OLD DOMINION

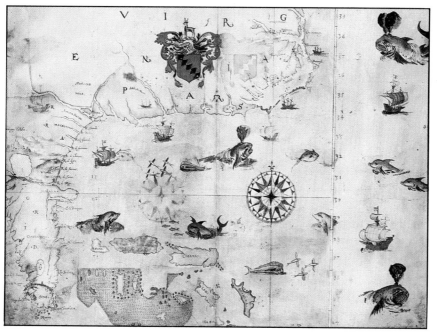

This map of the east coast of North America was
drawn by John White, an artist who sailed on Sir
Walter Raleigh's expedition to colonize Virginia
in 1585. Many of his sketches of Indians, plants,
and animals in the area were quite accurate.

When English explorers first set foot in Virginia, they encountered
Native Americans who had hunted its forests and farmed its valleys for
thousands of years. By 1607, England had established its first permanent
colony in the New World at Jamestown. Known as the "Old Dominion," the settlement survived many hard winters and eventually prospered. Virginia was a leader in the fight for independence from England
during the American Revolution. During the early 19th century, the
state's slave-based agricultural economy fell behind the more industrial-
ized North. As the nationwide debate over slavery grew, Virginians' loy-
alties were torn between the state and the federal government.

The Indians of Virginia

Like most other Native Americans, the first inhabitants of Virginia were descended from people who migrated from Asia thousands of years ago by crossing the Bering Strait, a land bridge that once connected Asia and North America. They were in search of big game that could provide them with food, clothing, and shelter. Over time, these people followed the animals southward and began to spread throughout North America.

The earliest known Native American site in Virginia dates back to 9500 B.C. Known as "Paleo" (or ancient)

Indians, these people were nomads who hunted animals such as bison, woolly mammoths, saber-toothed tigers, and American lions—all now extinct. They also gathered wild plants such as seeds, berries, and roots.

Gradually, over thousands of years, these Native Americans grouped into settlements, learned to farm, and

Shown here is a 19th-century engraving of an American bison, commonly known as the buffalo. Although the bison is most often associated with the Great Plains, there were substantial numbers east of the Mississippi River. Native Americans hunted bison using spears, and later, bows and arrows.

formed tribal societies ruled over by a single chief. They built large and elaborate villages that held hundreds, and even thousands, of people. They grew beans, corn, squash, and tobacco, and hunted wild game such as deer, turkey, bear, and rabbit.

In the period just before European contact, Virginia's Native Americans could be divided into three groups: the Mississippian Culture, who settled in the southwestern part of the region; the Earthen Mound Burial Culture in the Shenandoah Valley and the Piedmont (which is the area between the foothills of the Blue Ridge Mountains and the coastal plain); and the Coastal Plain Indians.

The Native Americans of the Mississippian Culture arrived in Virginia from the Tennessee and Ohio river valleys. They lived in large, walled settlements with complex societies that included chiefs, subchiefs, and priests. These settlements were often organized around one or more flat-topped pyramids (mounds), sometimes as tall as 100 feet, on which temples were built. The mounds were made of piled earth, and the stairways were made of logs. It was thought that the higher the mound was built, the closer the Native Americans could get to the spirit world.

Mississippian groups sometimes buried important members of their society, like chiefs and priests, in burial mounds, along with goods such as pottery and carvings. These mounds

The Indian village of Secotan, located on the Pamlico River, was visited by artist John White in 1586. Villagers in the foreground dance and participate in an annual feast, while in the background men hunt deer in the adjoining woods. White described the Indians in the town as people who lived "happily together without envy or greed."

were usually in the shape of an animal or human, or designed with a complex geometric pattern.

The Earthen Mound Burial Culture of the Shenandoah Valley and Piedmont also built burial mounds. However, they used their mounds as graves for hundreds of people. The mounds were built up slowly over the generations as people died. There are only a few left today because many were built in the floodplains of rivers and were washed away.

The lifeways of the Coastal Plain Indians depended heavily on water. They farmed the rich soils deposited by the major rivers, and also relied upon fish as a source of food. The Chesapeake Bay overflowed with fish like shad and sturgeon. Shellfish, such as oysters, mussels, and crabs, were also an important part of their diet. The shells were often used in daily life as utensils, ornaments, and ceremonial items, and were crushed to cover shelter floors.

By the time the Europeans arrived in Virginia, many of the weaker coastal tribes had been brought under the rule of a central chief, Wahunsunacock. He ruled over what the Euro-

peans called the Powhatan Confederacy—thirty-two sub-chiefdoms in 150 villages. The word "powhatan" means "chief" and was used by the colonists to refer to Wahunsunacock and his people.

The coastal regions had the largest Native American population in the state; to the west there were far fewer settlements. In the Piedmont, the Manahoacs lived near the present site of Fredericksburg, the Monacans lived near the falls of the James River, and the Occaneechis and Saponis lived on the Roanoke River. All of these groups eventually merged with larger tribes or else disappeared soon after contact with Europeans.

In the farthest part of what is present-day Virginia, in the area of the mountains and the Shenandoah Valley, there were few Native American tribes. The Cherokees, who were descendants of the mound-building Mississippians, lived in a distant corner of southwest Virginia. The Totelo people lived near the New River valley, but most of the land was used as a hunting area for the Shawnees, Susquehannocks, and Iroquois, who came down from Pennsylvania and New York.

The lives of Virginia's Native Americans were changed forever with the arrival of the first English settlers in 1607. The next several decades would see periods of both peace and war as the two cultures came into contact with each other.

The Coastal Plain Indians were skilled fishermen. This engraving shows the different methods they used to catch fish: In shallow water the Indians used spears made from sharp, hollow fish tails attached to the ends of reeds or long rods. From dugout canoes they dragged nets through the water. They also built traps from reeds or sticks to catch many fish at one time.

Jamestown

In the early 1580s, English soldiers and adventurers like Sir Walter Raleigh made several attempts to colonize Virginia, which was named after Queen Elizabeth I of England (who was called the "Virgin Queen" because she had never married). Despite major setbacks like the disappearance of a colony on Roanoke Island (called the Lost Colony because the only trace left behind was the mysterious word "Croatoan" carved into a tree), the English were determined to stake a claim in North America. Their goal was to search for any riches the unknown land might hold, to spread Christianity among the Native Americans, and to prevent their rival, Spain, from founding more colonies in the New World.

In 1606, King James I granted a charter to settle in Virginia to a group of investors called the Virginia Company. In December of that year, 144 men and boys in three ships, the *Susan Constant*, the *Godspeed*, and the *Discovery*, set sail from London. The following April, they landed at Cape Henry on the Virginia coast.

From there, they sailed up the Chesapeake Bay and entered the mouth of a large river, which they named the James, in honor of their king. On May 13, they chose a small peninsula upon which to build their

Building a fort to protect the colonists from hostile Native Americans and Spanish attack was one of the first and most important tasks at Jamestown. The soldier posted at left is probably standing guard against Indians—although he could have been there to make sure that everyone did an equal amount of work.

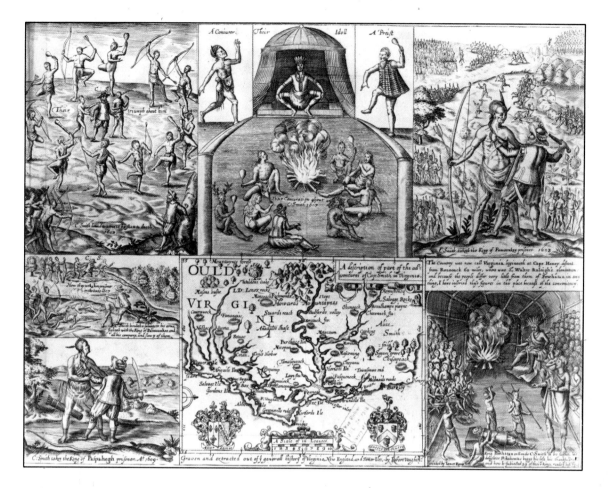

fort. Called Jamestown, it was the first permanent English colony in America.

The site, while easy to defend, turned out to be a poor choice. It was low and swampy, making it the perfect breeding ground for mosquitos that carried diseases such as malaria. By the end of the summer nearly half of the men were either dead or dying from fever. Few of the settlers knew how to farm or had the skills necessary to survive in the wilderness. Crops were not planted in time for winter, and if not for some friendly Native Americans who shared their corn, the settlers would have starved.

Not all of the Indians were friendly, however. Jamestown was often attacked by Native Americans who were angry at the Englishmen's presence

Captain John Smith drew this series of pictures showing his adventures in Virginia. In the top panels, Smith is shown capturing and being captured by Indian chiefs; in the lower right panel, Pocahontas begs her father, Chief Powhatan, to spare Smith's life. Smith was thought to have exaggerated about many of his exploits.

on their land. In December, Captain John Smith was kidnapped by Chief Powhatan, then ruler of the Powhatan Confederacy. He was held for several days but released after Powhatan's daughter, Pocahontas, pleaded for his life.

Smith was a councilman, one of a group of colonists who ran the daily affairs of the colony for the Virginia Company. By September 1608, he had become president of the council. Smith was a strict leader who felt that every colonist, nobleman or not, should work for the benefit of the group. He was often heard saying, "he that will not worke, shall not eate." By the fall of 1609, the settlers had harvested their first crop of corn.

During Smith's year as leader, two important events occurred. In October 1608, the first women arrived in Jamestown—Mrs. Forrest and her maid, Anne Burras. And, in May 1609, King James granted the Virginia Company a new charter, which gave them control over a much larger area—200 miles north and south of Jamestown and an indefinite distance

As a private business owned by investors, the Virginia Company's main purpose was to make a profit, and this success depended on attracting as many colonists as possible. This 1609 poster, circulated in London, advertises excellent farming at Jamestown.

King James I is pictured on the front of the seal of the Virginia Company of London. It was he who granted the company permission to establish the colony at Jamestown.

west. The new charter also gave the company the power to appoint the council, which in turn named the governor for the colony.

By late summer, a group of 300 men, women, and children arrived in Jamestown from England, bringing the total population to 500. In September, Smith, who had been accidentally wounded in the leg by exploding gunpowder, left for England. He never returned.

Although the new settlers, many of whom arrived with tools and seeds, were better prepared to combat the harshness of life in the wilderness, the winter of 1609 proved disastrous. Bitter cold weather and a siege by the Powhatans (which cut the colonists off from a storage area full of supplies) left all but sixty settlers dead. It was a winter that came to be known as "the Starving Time."

When acting governor Sir Thomas Gates arrived with additional settlers in May 1610, the situation was so desperate that he decided to pack up the whole colony and leave. However, on their way down the James River, they ran into an arriving supply ship under new governor Lord De La Warr, who ordered them to turn back.

The Jamestown colony had nearly failed. Under De La Warr, and later Sir Thomas Dale, conditions began to improve. Hundreds of new settlers—strong, willing workers—arrived in 1611 and set about rebuilding the town. Like their predecessor, John

Sir Walter Raleigh made smoking tobacco popular in England after 1586. But because King James (who hated smoking) refused to grow it in England, demand for the plant gave Virginia its first and most important cash crop.

Smith, both De La Warr and Dale expected hard work and discipline from the colonists.

In 1613, Pocahontas, the daughter of Chief Powhatan, was captured by the English and held prisoner in order to get the Powhatans to stop attacking the settlement. While at Jamestown, she and a settler named John Rolfe fell in love. Their marriage in 1614 brought eight years of peace between the Indians and the English.

Rolfe is credited with developing the colony's first major product—a mild, sweeter tobacco that soon became popular in England. By 1619, it was the colony's biggest cash crop and would remain the backbone of Virginia's economy for more than 200 years.

In August 1619, a Dutch ship brought twenty Africans to Jamestown. Kidnapped from their homes by slave traders, they had been sold to the Spanish to work in their colonies in the West Indies. They were then captured by the Dutch and sold to the Jamestown settlers as indentured servants allowed to work to earn their freedom.

By 1622, the colony finally seemed to be flourishing. Small tobacco farms sprang up along the York and James

This painting by Howard Pyle shows the arrival of the first Africans in Jamestown in 1619. While they were considered indentured servants rather than slaves (allowing them to work for their freedom), a law was passed in 1662 that made all African Americans servants for life. By 1681, most of the 3,000 African Americans in Virginia were considered slaves.

rivers. But on March 22, 1622, the Powhatans launched a surprise attack on the outer edges of the colony. Under the leadership of Opechancanough, Powhatan's successor, they killed 347 people—nearly a third of the total population.

The uprising was eventually put down, but the continued unrest in Virginia worried King James. On May 24, 1624, he revoked the Virginia Company's charter and brought the colony under royal control.

A Royal Colony

In the beginning, the change to royal rule had little effect on the colony. Instead of the Virginia Company, the king now appointed the royal governor. In turn, the governor named a council to advise him. The council was made up of many of the same wealthy planters who were councilmen before royal rule. They sat in the upper house of the General Assembly and also served as the General Court. The House of Burgesses, which was made up of representatives from Virginia's counties, sat in the lower house. They had the power to make laws and raise taxes, all upon approval of the king.

In January 1625, only 1,232 people lived in the Virginia colony. Disease killed many, and life was still very difficult, but conditions were improving. Relations with the Powhatans were peaceful, and a hard-working farmer could prosper by raising tobacco. As life became more stable, new settlers decided to seek their fortunes in Virginia and the colony grew.

The opportunity to own land drew many Englishmen to Virginia. For others, it was a chance to start a new

By the mid-1600s, the tobacco trade between Virginia and England was flourishing. To protect the tobacco leaves during shipping, tobacco growers packed them into barrels nearly four feet tall and, when filled, weighing as much as 475 pounds. This painting shows three men struggling to roll one of the barrels up a gangplank onto a merchant vessel.

life in a society that was less restrictive than England's. Even indentured servants, who had to work (usually for seven years) to earn their freedom, could become landowners and respected members of society.

The colony still centered on Jamestown, but it was steadily expanding along the banks of the James River. Most of the farms were relatively small and isolated. Tobacco, which was in great demand in England, was by far the most profitable crop grown. (In fact, it came to be known as "green gold," because it was so valuable that it was often used just like money in exchange for goods.) However, the colony's heavy dependence on one crop was very risky because a drop in prices could mean financial ruin for a farmer.

Virginia had very few towns and villages because most people lived and worked on farms. Just as in England, the county was the basic unit of local government. Each county had judges who made up the local court. The court met once a month so that people from outlying areas could attend. The person responsible for enforcing the law was the sheriff. All county officers were appointed by the governor.

By 1635, the colony's population had grown to about 5,000 people in eight counties. Virginia's boundaries had been reduced, however. In 1629, the province of North Carolina was carved out of the southern part of the colony, and in 1632, Maryland was created from lands in the colony's northern region.

Despite the loss of territory, the colony was prosperous. In 1642, when Sir William Berkeley became governor, the population had increased to 15,000 whites and 300 blacks. Two years later, on April 18, 1644, the Indians of the Powhatan Confederacy made one last desperate attempt to drive away the English. Led once again by Opechancanough, now an old man, the Powhatans massacred 350 settlers. Berkeley responded quickly with force. Within three years, the Powhatan Confederacy lay in ruins, and Opechancanough was forced to surrender. After signing a peace treaty, the two sides lived in relative harmony for the next thirty years.

While the colonist's relationship with the Powhatans improved, relations with England were becoming increasingly tense. In 1661, King Charles II imposed the Navigation Acts, which required Virginians to export their tobacco only on English ships bound for England. Moreover, there was too much tobacco on the market and attempts to limit production were declared illegal by the Crown. Prices plummeted, driving many small farmers out of business. As a result, huge plantations developed in their place.

Large plantations were more profitable because the owners could use slave labor to grow greater amounts of tobacco. Slavery was legalized in

the colony in 1661, and by 1670 there were nearly 2,000 slaves in Virginia. That same year the General Assembly restricted the right to vote to men who owned land or houses. Previously, all freemen could vote, and many people were angry that this right was taken away from them.

Meanwhile, more people were pushing into the western part of the region and settling among the rolling hills and along the James and Rappahannock rivers. In the early 1670s, explorers like John Lederer and Abraham Wood crossed the barrier of the

In this sketch, the body of Powhatan chief Opechancanough is carried through the streets of Jamestown for burial. Governor William Berkeley had planned to take the defeated leader of the 1644 Indian uprising to England, but an angry soldier shot the chief in revenge for the massacre of 350 settlers.

Blue Ridge Mountains and looked out upon the Valley of Virginia and to the Allegheny Mountains in the west.

In 1675, conflict erupted between the Susquehannock tribe and new settlers on the western edge of the colony. When thirty-six people were killed in Stafford County, the settlers demanded immediate action from the governor. Governor Berkeley (who had been restored as head of the colony in 1660) declared war on the Susquehannocks and ordered forts to be built on the western frontier. After a series of skirmishes, the tribe let it be known that they were ready for peace. Berkeley agreed to call off the war.

On June 23, 1676, the rebel Nathaniel Bacon, accompanied by many of his well-armed followers, confronted Governor Berkeley in Jamestown and demanded permission to lead his forces against attacking Indians. This engraving (below) shows Berkeley (on the left) refusing Bacon's request and opening his coat in response, daring the rebels to shoot him. Despite Berkeley's show of courage, Bacon and his militia burned Jamestown in September.

This enraged the settlers in the western part of the colony who were afraid that the Native Americans would continue to attack. They reasoned that Berkeley stopped the war because he did not care about protecting them. In April 1676, a young planter named Nathaniel Bacon raised a force to rise up against the Native Americans. Berkeley refused to grant him permission to fight, but Bacon ignored him and marched off into the wilderness. He fought and defeated a party of Susquehannocks and Occaneechees on the banks of the Roanoke River.

Berkeley declared Bacon a traitor and ordered his arrest. Soon Bacon and his followers were in open rebellion against the governor. Throughout the summer, Bacon's forces fought the governor's army, and at one point had Berkeley in retreat to the Eastern Shore. They burned Jamestown in September and seemed to be on the verge of victory when Bacon died of fever in October.

Without Bacon's leadership, the rebellion quickly fell apart. Berkeley regained control of the colony and hanged several of the rebels. Bacon's Rebellion was short-lived but it was significant because it showed that the colonists' interests were often different from those of the king. Nearly 100 years later, a much larger rebellion would result in the American Revolution.

A New Century and New Prosperity

Following Bacon's Rebellion, Berkeley left Virginia. In his place, a series of governors were sent to the colony to keep order and to make sure that the colonists did not try to prevent tobacco from being shipped to England. In 1688, William and Mary became the king and queen of England, and in 1693 they granted a charter for Virginia's first university—the College of William and Mary.

In 1699, the colonial capital was moved from Jamestown to a spot several miles up the James River called Williamsburg. By the turn of the century, Virginia's population was 58,000

Spotswood's journey into the wilderness with his Knights of the Golden Horseshoe lasted four weeks and covered 438 miles. When they finally reached the summit of Shenandoah Mountain, the "knights" toasted the king's health with champagne and were each presented a golden horseshoe by Spotswood to remember the event.

and growing. During Governor Alexander Spotswood's administration (1710–22), the frontier opened up, especially after he and a few companions crossed the Blue Ridge Mountains and explored the Shenandoah Valley. They called themselves the Knights of the Golden Horseshoe, and tales of their adventures captured the public's imagination.

With tobacco bringing a better price in England, plantations expanded and slavery increased. Growing tobacco required large amounts of land and a big labor force, and using slaves was believed to be the cheapest way to plant and harvest the crop.

William Gooch became governor of Virginia in 1727, the beginning of the so-called Golden Age of plantation society. During Gooch's twenty-two-year administration, the colony grew to forty-four counties stretching across the Blue Ridge Mountains and up the Valley of Virginia.

Wealthy Tidewater planter families like the Carters, Randolphs, and Byrds built huge mansions on plantations of many thousands of acres. They were often hard-working, industrious members of society and felt that education and the arts were both very important.

The Piedmont region developed as new towns were founded on major rivers—Richmond on the James, Fredericksburg on the Rappahannock, Petersburg on the Appomattox, and Alexandria on the Potomac. Wealthy planters bought up huge tracts of fertile land to grow tobacco, and soon there were more plantations in the Piedmont than in the Tidewater.

West of the Blue Ridge Mountains, the Valley region was settled in the 1730s and 1740s. The mountains were barriers to settlers in the eastern part of Virginia, so most of the immigrants were Scottish-Irish and German who moved south from Pennsylvania into the Shenandoah Valley. They

Mt. Vernon was typical of many Virginia plantations built by wealthy tobacco planters. Famous as the home of George Washington, the structure dates to before 1700. After he inherited the house in 1752 from his half-brother, Washington gradually enlarged it.

owned small farms and grew grains like wheat and corn rather than tobacco. They owned few slaves.

Most of these settlers were Presbyterians, Congregationalists, or members of other religions. They were called "dissenters" because they had broken away from the Anglican Church, which was the official church in Virginia. Nevertheless, the valley settlers were tolerated because they protected settlers in the eastern part of the colony from the Indians and French in the west.

In the 1750s, the French and English clashed over control of the Ohio River territory in the French and Indian War. In 1755, a British force under the command of Major General Edward Braddock was defeated by the French at Fort Duquesne (present-

In 1755, George Washington (on horseback) was a twenty-three-year-old lieutenant colonel in the colonial militia and aide to English general Edward Braddock. In the battle pictured here against French and Indian forces, Washington led the wounded Braddock's defeated troops to safety. He was later promoted to commander-in-chief of all Virginia forces.

day Pittsburgh). Braddock was killed, but a young lieutenant colonel in the colonial militia named George Washington survived. For the next three years, Washington defended Virginia's western frontier from raids by Native Americans. The tide turned against the French in 1758, and a larger British army, including Washington's Virginia militia, captured Fort Duquesne. Thereafter, the French and Indians were no longer a threat to Virginia.

Discontent and Revolution

A series of events in the 1750s and 1760s began to turn the settlers against the British government. In many cases, the English challenged and overturned laws passed by the Virginia General Assembly and declared them illegal. Angry Virginians thought that the king should not meddle in what they considered their internal affairs, especially when it came to taxing the colonists.

In an attempt to keep peace between settlers and Native Americans, Parliament passed the Proclamation of 1763 making all land west of the Allegheny Mountains off limits to settlement. However, the proclamation proved unenforceable and most settlers simply ignored it. They had fought to keep this area, known as Kentucky, from the French during the French and Indian War. Besides, they reasoned, the Charter of 1609 gave the land to Virginia, and England had no right to keep them away from it.

The first major sign of discontent came in 1765 following the passage of the Stamp Act, which required colonists to buy stamps for printed materials. Through this act, the English tried taxing the colonies to help pay for the recent war and the cost of maintaining a large army in America.

A recently elected member of the House of Burgesses, Patrick Henry, declared in his famous Stamp Act Resolves that Virginia's General Assembly was the only political body with a right to tax the Virginia people. Virginia (and the other colonies) rallied around Henry, and within a year Parliament canceled the act.

Still convinced of its power to tax the American colonies, the English government passed the Townshend Acts in 1767. The acts taxed many products coming from England, including tea. The British wanted to use this tax money to pay their officials working in the colonies. Virginia, joined by Massachusetts, refused to buy English goods on the principle that it was illegal for the English government to make laws regarding the colonies when the colonies had no part in the decisions that were made.

The other colonies followed Virginia's lead, and in 1770 Parliament stopped taxing everything except tea. Virginians declared their sympathy with the Massachusetts colony after the Boston Tea Party in late 1773, in which colonists dumped 342 chests of tea into Boston Harbor. Alarmed by the growing unrest, Virginia's governor Dunmore, who was appointed by the English government, dissolved the General Assembly and placed Virginia entirely under British rule.

The colonists ignored England's decision, and the assembly met in August 1774 at Raleigh Tavern in Williamsburg. After contacting the other colonies, the Virginia Convention made plans to send representatives to the first Continental Congress in Philadelphia. Those chosen to represent Virginia were Peyton Randolph, George Washington, Patrick Henry, Richard Henry Lee, Edmund Pendleton, Richard Bland, and Benjamin Harrison.

A second convention met in St. John's Church in Richmond in March 1775. The more radical members of the convention, led by Patrick Henry, wanted to raise a militia to defend themselves. It was here that Henry gave his famous speech that ended with the passionate words, "I know not what course others may take; but as for me, give me liberty, or give me death!"

A few weeks later, the first shots of the Revolutionary War were fired at Lexington and Concord in Massachusetts. Virginia governor Dunmore fled to a ship waiting in the York River. At the second Continental Congress in Philadelphia that June, George Washington was chosen to command the Continental Army.

On May 15, 1776, the Virginia Convention met in Williamsburg to instruct its delegates to the Continental Congress to vote for independence from England. The convention chose Patrick Henry to be the first governor of the Commonwealth of Virginia and adopted a state constitution and bill of

In his early years, Patrick Henry attempted both farming and store keeping, and failed at both. He went on to become a successful lawyer and one of the greatest speakers in colonial Virginia. Here he addresses the General Assembly.

rights (which was the model for the federal bill of rights a few years later).

In Philadelphia on June 7, Richard Henry Lee proposed in the Virginia Resolution that the colonies declare themselves free. Thomas Jefferson, a thirty-three-year-old resident of Albemarle County, drafted the Declaration of Independence. It was adopted on July 4, 1776.

The war did not reach Virginia until 1780, although Virginians like Daniel Morgan's western riflemen, Henry

"Light Horse Harry" Lee's cavalry, and George Rogers Clark's force in the Northwest Territory all played major roles in the conflict from the beginning. Recently elected Governor Jefferson moved the capital from Williamsburg to Richmond to keep it out of the hands of the British forces under the command of General Charles Cornwallis. Aided by Benedict Arnold, an American spying for England, the British burned Richmond in 1781 and advanced as far west as Charlottesville.

However, Continental forces, with French help, forced Cornwallis to retreat to Yorktown, a small town on the Virginia coast. Washington brought in reinforcements, and on October 19, 1781, Cornwallis surrendered. The last battle of the Revolution was fought on Virginia soil.

This lithograph shows the British surrender at Yorktown on October 19, 1781. After an eleven-day siege by American and French forces, General Cornwallis found himself surrounded on all sides and admitted defeat. As the British troops marched away from Yorktown, the American band broke into "Yankee Doodle" to celebrate their victory.

A Leading Role in a New Nation

After the Revolution, Virginia was the largest state in the new nation. Based on the Charter of 1609 and Clark's capture of the Northwest Territory from the British, the state stretched to present-day Wisconsin. Several smaller states, such as Maryland, worried that Virginia's size and population, now more than 500,000, would make it too powerful in the new central government of the United States.

In 1781, Virginia put these fears to rest by giving up more than 250,000 square miles of land and any claim to the Northwest Territory. Virginia remained the largest state, but it was easier to govern and less threatening to the other states.

The Northwest Ordinance of 1787 stated that new states admitted to the Union would be equal to the original thirteen states in all respects, with the same rights and privileges. At Jefferson's request, slavery was banned in the Northwest Territory. Ohio, Indiana, Illinois, Michigan, and Wisconsin were eventually carved from this vast area. Kentucky requested separation from Virginia in 1786 and became the fifteenth state in 1792.

In the years following the Revolution, it became evident that the Articles of Confederation gave too much power to the states and too little to the federal government. Virginians such as James Madison took the lead in calling for a constitutional convention of all the states to revise the Articles of Confederation.

Madison, joined by Alexander Hamilton of New York, succeeded in organizing the Constitutional Convention of Philadelphia in May 1787. Virginia named George Washington to head its delegation, which included some of the state's most noted leaders, such as Madison himself, George Mason, Edmund Randolph, and George Wythe. Absent were Jefferson, who was in France, and Patrick Henry, who believed that a new constitution would give too much power to the federal government.

After the Constitution was signed by a majority of the delegates, it had to be approved by at least nine of the thirteen states. Given Virginia's leading role in the new republic, the Virginia Convention's decision was eagerly awaited. On June 26, 1788, after much heated debate, Virginia became the tenth state to approve the Constitution of the United States.

George Washington, a native of Westmoreland County, Virginia, was elected unanimously as the first president of the United States. A Revolutionary War hero, he was without a doubt the most respected figure in the country. He chose two Virginians to be in his cabinet: Thomas Jefferson as secretary of state and Edmund Randolph as attorney general.

Washington served two terms as

president, from 1789–97. During his presidency, Congress passed ten amendments to the Constitution, including the Bill of Rights. Washington's presidency was also marked by the development of the first political parties. The Federalists, led by Secretary of the Treasury Alexander Hamilton, wanted a strong national government and closer ties with England. The Jeffersonian Republicans, led by Jefferson and Madison, wanted to concentrate government on the state and local level and to maintain good relations with France.

These two parties became increasingly hostile to each other. Most of Virginia was strongly Republican, but the growing cities of Richmond and Norfolk sympathized with the Federalists. Washington himself supported the Federalists, although he was careful to stay out of party politics.

In 1796, Virginian Thomas Jefferson, Washington's former secretary of state, won election as vice president of

George Washington only reluctantly accepted his appointment as the first president of the United States. In April 1789, in a letter to his friend, Henry Knox, he wrote, "my movements to the chair of Government will be accompanied by feelings not unlike those of a culprit . . . going to the place of his execution." This engraving shows Washington at Mount Vernon.

the United States. Four years later he narrowly defeated President John Adams in the presidential election, beginning a twenty-four-year reign of Virginians in the White House.

Jefferson served two terms in office. In his first term, the United States bought a huge piece of land from France called the Louisiana Purchase, doubling the size of the country. Jefferson sent an expedition headed by two Virginians, Meriwether Lewis and William Clark, to explore the territory. They discovered an overland route to the Pacific Ocean, returning with a great deal of scientific information collected on their journey.

During Jefferson's second term, the war between England and France created tension in the United States when American sailors captured on the high seas were forced to serve in the British Navy. Jefferson tried to remain neutral, but the public wanted war.

His successor, James Madison, declared war on England in 1812. Although most of the fighting occurred to the north in Canada, New York, and Pennsylvania, on numerous occasions Virginians were called upon to defend their towns. In June 1813, the British attempted to capture Norfolk, but a small band of Virginians waiting for them on an island at the mouth of the Elizabeth River forced them to retreat. The town of Hampton, located across the James River from Norfolk, was not so fortunate. The British were able to attack and easily defeat the small force stationed there.

One of the greatest economic hardships suffered by Virginia during the war was the British blockade of the port of Norfolk. This blockade prevented goods from being shipped to the state. In addition, the Americans set up an embargo preventing goods from being shipped out of the port, which was meant to stop American cargo from falling into British hands. Norfolk's shipping industry was devestated, and it did not fully recover until the end of the war.

Of all of Thomas Jefferson's achievements, the three he was most proud of were recorded on his tombstone: " . . . author of the Declaration of American Independence, of the Virginia Statute for Religious Freedom, and father of the University of Virginia."

Political Tension and Sectionalism

For more than twenty-five years, Virginians dominated national politics. All of these men were Jeffersonian Republicans who believed that individual states should have more control over the law than the federal government. Jefferson and his followers also spoke on behalf of the interests of the common citizen, believing that leadership should be based on an ability to lead rather than on the amount of money a person had.

Jefferson founded the University of Virginia in Charlottesville in 1819. He designed many of the buildings on campus and considered it his proudest achievement. That same year, Virginia was hard hit by the Great Panic, a nationwide depression that caused the price of tobacco and other crops to drop sharply. Years of tobacco harvesting east of the Blue Ridge Mountains had taken away the nutrients from the soil and made it difficult to grow anything. As a result, many Virginians could not make a liv-

Shown here is an early 1800s engraving of the front lawn of the University of Virginia in Charlottesville, with the rotunda in the background. Jefferson surveyed the site, drew up plans for the buildings, and designed the university's course of study. In 1825, just one year before his death, "Mr. Jefferson's University" opened its doors.

This photograph shows a recently branded slave bound in chains with a restraining choker around his neck. Few owners mistreated their slaves in everyday life—they were too valuable as property. But punishment for even minor offenses could be severe. A slave's life was defined by two things: constant work and a complete lack of freedom.

ing and simply left the area—moving to Kentucky, Tennessee, and other states south of the Ohio River valley. For the first time since its founding, Virginia's population declined.

By 1825, tensions were beginning to grow between the eastern and western halves of the state. The barrier created by the Blue Ridge Mountains made travel and communication difficult, and western Virginians believed that they did not have enough say in state politics. In 1816, they met in Staunton to demand a new constitution that better reflected their growing region.

In 1829, a constitutional convention was held in Richmond to address the westerners' grievances. Their delegates argued for the vote to be given to all white taxpayers (not just property holders) and for an equal say in state government. The eastern delegates allowed some changes, broadening the vote to include leaseholders and householders, and creating more seats in the General Assembly to represent western interests. The constitution was ratified in 1830, but few westerners were satisfied with the outcome.

The issue of slavery also divided the state. There were fewer slaveholders west of the Blue Ridge Mountains and many of the independent small farmers of that region favored the abolition (elimination) of slavery. Most Virginians knew that slavery was morally wrong, but it had be-

come such a part of life in the state that no one could design a workable plan to end the practice. As it came under increasing attack from Northern abolitionists, Virginians were forced to come up with elaborate arguments in defense of a practice that, in the end, was impossible to defend.

Nearly all talk of abolishing slavery ceased after a rebellion led by the slave Nat Turner in 1831. On August 22, he and a group of about sixty slaves and free blacks rose up and killed Turner's second master, Joseph Travis, and his wife and infant child. For two days, they rampaged through Southampton County, murdering fifty-eight whites, before the rebellion collapsed. Turner hid in the swamps for several weeks before he was captured.

Turner's revolt created great fear

This woodcut portrays, inaccurately, the August 1831 revolt led by the slave Nat Turner. In the early 1820s, Turner was sold to a man, Joseph Travis, who no longer allowed him to continue his education. Angry and frustrated, he became convinced that he was destined to lead blacks out of slavery. His bloody uprising failed, and many innocent African Americans were in turn murdered by whites in revenge. Turner was eventually caught, tried, and hanged.

among Virginia's white population. When it was learned that Turner could read and write and had been treated kindly by his first master, Benjamin Turner, public opinion turned against freeing the slaves. A bill to abolish slavery, introduced in the General Assembly in 1832, was defeated. For the next thirty years, slavery remained an ugly fact of life in the Old Dominion.

The 1840s was a decade of relative prosperity. Railroads boosted Virginia's economy by linking different parts of the state. Richmond became the distribution point for the state's tobacco crop as well as a manufacturing center. The Tredegar Iron Works was the largest iron foundry in the entire South.

The 1850s began on a hopeful note but ended badly. In the new state constitution of 1851, all white males were given the right to vote, and the western counties won better representation in the General Assembly. On October 16, 1859, a small band of men led by abolitionist John Brown seized the federal arsenal at Harpers Ferry in northwestern Virginia. He intended to use the arms for a planned slave revolt. U.S. troops under the command of Colonel Robert E. Lee were sent in to capture him.

Brown was caught, tried, and hanged for treason. His death inflamed passions in the North and South—passions that would soon explode into war.

In this mythical painting, John Brown calls upon the nation to rise up against slavery. While some people considered him crazy, Brown was convinced that he had been appointed by God to free the slaves.

PART TWO

THE NEW DOMINION

Virginia statesman George Mason designed the floorplan and the exterior of Gunston Hall, his plantation on the Potomac River. This photograph shows an aerial view of the house, along with the formal gardens and deer park.

The Civil War, the bloodiest conflict in American history, was fought almost entirely on Virginia soil. After the war, Virginia was devastated, its land and economy destroyed. For several years under Reconstruction, the state suffered under military rule. Recovery was slow, but by the late 19th century, Virginia was once again prosperous. A revised state constitution in 1902 instituted taxes and other restrictions that largely affected African Americans. Both World Wars stimulated industrial growth and Virginia became more urbanized. Official segregation of the races lasted until the late 1950s. Virginians in the 1990s are increasingly challenged to keep their rich historical heritage alive as the state moves into the next century.

The Civil War

As the national debate over slavery grew ever more bitter, Virginia tried to take a moderate position. While there were many Virginians who saw slavery as a necessary evil, there were few "fire eaters" (extremists who passionately defended slavery and wanted to break away from the Union) in the Deep South.

On the other hand, most Virginians resented attacks from the equally extreme abolitionists to the north. They believed that the problem of slavery should be dealt with by the state, without interference from the federal government. In addition, Virginia's leaders believed in a state's right to secede (split from the Union) if forced to do so.

After John Brown's raid, events spun rapidly out of control. The presidential election of 1860 divided the nation along pro- and antislavery lines. The Democratic Party (formerly the Jeffersonian Republicans) split into northern and southern halves and chose separate candidates— Stephen Douglas in the North, Vice President John C. Breckinridge in the South. A new party calling itself the Republicans, dedicated to ending slavery, or at least preventing its spread, nominated Abraham Lincoln. Virginians voted primarily for Tennessee's John Bell, head of the moderate Constitutional Union Party.

After Lincoln was elected, South Carolina carried out its threat to break away from the Union. Six other Deep South states quickly followed. Virginia, in an attempt to hold the nation together, called for a convention of the states in Washington in February. It was too late. On April 12, 1861, Confederate cannons fired on Fort Sumter in South Carolina's Charleston Harbor. Ironically, it was a Virginian, Edmund Ruffin, who fired the first shot of the war.

Edmund Ruffin (1794–1865) was first known as an agricultural pioneer who developed ways to improve the South's worn-out soil. Later, he became a "fire eater," calling for Virginia's secession from the Union. Credited with firing the first shot of the Civil War, he committed suicide soon after the South's defeat in 1865.

In this wood engraving, Confederate president Jefferson Davis (1808–89) and his cabinet speak with General Robert E. Lee in the council chambers at Richmond, the Confederate capital. Many people left the Confederate cabinet during the war—Davis went through three secretaries of state and six secretaries of war.

When Lincoln called for troops from all the states to put down the rebellion, Virginia voted to secede rather than fight against another Southern state. On April 25, Virginia joined the Confederate States of America.

The Old Dominion assumed a leading role in the Confederacy when the capital was moved from Montgomery, Alabama, to Richmond in May 1861. Confederate president Jefferson Davis appointed Robert E. Lee commander of Virginia's forces. Within a year, he headed the entire Army of Northern Virginia which included all Confederate troops that fought in the state. Lee, who had served in the U.S. Army with distinction in the Mexican War and had been the superintendent at West Point, had turned down Lincoln's offer to command the federal army. He could not bring himself to invade his native state, choosing instead to fight with Virginia.

Lee immediately set about raising an army and gathering a staff of officers. One of his generals was Thomas Jonathan Jackson, an unknown professor from the Virginia Military Institute in Lexington. Another was a twenty-nine-year-old cavalryman named J.E.B. Stuart. The two men could not have been more different: Jackson was a strange, grimly religious man who liked to suck on lemons; Stuart, a flamboyant horseman with a trademark plumed hat. They would prove to be two of Lee's most brilliant officers.

Most Americans, North and South, believed the war would last no more than a few months. The First Battle of Manassas on July 21, 1861, proved that assumption wrong. Just as the Confederates seemed on the verge of being defeated by a larger Northern force, a fleeing South Carolina general noticed Jackson standing firm. "There stands Jackson like a stone wall!" he cried. "Rally behind the Virginians!" Defeat turned to victory and Union troops fled back to Washington, trailed by panicked sightseers who had come to watch the battle. "Stonewall" Jackson had earned his nickname and there would be nearly four more years of bloody fighting.

Lee was outnumbered from the beginning. The Union forces were better equipped and supplied. He knew that his only hope was to out-maneuver the enemy long enough for the North to grow tired of war. There was also a chance of English or French support if the Confederacy showed it could win in battle. For the first two years of the war, it looked as if Lee's bold scheme might work.

He knew, too, that he had to keep Richmond out of enemy hands. Early in 1862, Union troops under the command of George McClellan marched to within sight of the city.

Faced with superior numbers, Lee was able to hold Richmond, thanks in large part to Jackson and Stuart's dazzling performances.

In the Shenandoah Valley, Jackson kept Union reinforcements away from Richmond by waging one of the most remarkable campaigns in military history. With lightning-fast movements, he defeated two Union armies with a force one-third their size, and drove them all the way to the Potomac River before joining Lee. After Jackson's Valley campaign, his troops were

In the confused night of fighting at Chancellorsville, Stonewall Jackson was accidentally shot in the left arm by his own troops. Although he was expected to recover, Jackson became weak and died of pneumonia eight days later.

called "foot cavalry" because of the incredible distances they could cover in a short time.

Meanwhile, Stuart's cavalry performed the amazing feat of riding completely around McClellan's army. For days, Lee's "eyes and ears" relayed information while escaping capture. Lee forced McClellan to retreat and Richmond was saved, although at a terrible cost to the Confederacy. In the Seven Days' Battles, Lee lost 11,000 of his best men and failed to destroy the Union Army, which regrouped for another invasion.

At the Second Battle of Manassas in August, Lee again defeated the Union Army, capturing valuable supplies and ammunition. With the Old Dominion free of Northern armies, Lee took the offensive and mounted an invasion of his own. In September, he crossed the Potomac into Maryland.

The Battle of Sharpsburg on September 17 was a turning point in the war. Lee fought McClellan's troops to a draw and both sides suffered terrible losses. His exhausted, hungry army was forced to withdraw into Virginia. Lee's failure to carry the war onto Northern soil at Sharpsburg meant no foreign help for the Confederacy.

Back in Virginia, in the winter and spring of 1862–63, Lee proved nearly unbeatable. He inflicted horrible casualties against Ambrose Burnside at Fredericksburg in mid-December. In May, during the Battle of Chancellorsville, Stonewall Jackson was accidentally shot by one of his own men. His death was a terrible loss for the Confederacy.

A month later, Lee made one last attempt to invade the North. The three-day battle near the small Pennsylvania town of Gettysburg was the bloodiest in American history. Some

50,000 men on both sides were killed or wounded. Three thousand Virginians went down in Pickett's Charge alone. Lee, his army in tatters, retreated once more across the Potomac into Virginia.

The next two years saw Lee fighting an increasingly defensive war as Union general Ulysses S. Grant tightened his grip around the shrinking Army of Northern Virginia. Incredibly, with few men and dwindling supplies, Lee still inflicted heavy casualties on Union troops.

During the Wilderness Campaign, carried out in May–June 1864, Lee repeatedly escaped from Grant's clutches, always keeping himself between the Union Army and Richmond. At the Battle of Cold Harbor on June 3, more than 7,000 Union troops were killed or wounded in less than thirty minutes.

A determined Grant changed his strategy and dug in his troops, laying siege to the cities of Petersburg and Richmond through the fall and winter. Meanwhile, Union general Philip Sheridan ravaged the Shenandoah Valley, cutting off Lee's food supply.

Grant's plan worked. Richmond fell on April 2, 1865, and Lee, surrounded with no hope of escape, surrendered seven days later at Appomattox Court House near Lynchburg, Virginia. The war was over.

Two women in black walk past the charred ruins of a building in Richmond. Shortly before the city's fall on April 2, 1865, retreating Confederate forces set fire to military warehouses and supplies, and whole neighborhoods in the business district burned to the ground.

Reconstruction and Revival

Virginia lay in ruins after the Civil War. Four years of heavy fighting had ended in defeat, leaving physical and emotional scars that would take years to heal. Railroads were destroyed, fields lay empty, cities were reduced to piles of rubble, and a whole generation of young men was lost. The financial losses to the Old Dominion were estimated at $457 million.

During the war, Virginia lost nearly a third of its territory when the area between the Alleghenies and the Ohio River broke away to form the state of West Virginia in 1863. That same year, President Lincoln's Emancipation Proclamation freed the slaves in the Confederate states. After the war, Virginia's 350,000 former slaves were left with their freedom, but little else.

Francis H. Pierpoint, who headed Virginia's provisional (or Northern-recognized) government during the war, was given the responsibility for rebuilding the state's political system. After a statewide election in October, 1865, Virginia's delegation to Congress was given a hostile reception by the Radical Republicans.

It was very difficult for freed slaves to get fair treatment from their white employers after the war. As a result, the federal government established the Freedman's Bureau in 1865, which, among other things, enforced labor contracts and saw to it that black workers were not abused or exploited on the job. A group of black laborers on a riverfront dock posed for this photograph in post-Civil War Virginia.

William Mahone first came into prominence as a Confederate major general at the Battle of the Crater during the Civil War. He began his fifteen-year reign over Virginia politics in the early 1870s, and during that time worked to improve the state's public school system for African Americans as well as whites.

Members of this party wanted to make it very difficult for the former Confederate states to be readmitted to the Union. Part of their plan—Reconstruction—called for ratification of the Fourteenth Amendment as a necessary step for statehood. This amendment gave African Americans their citizenship but it also prevented former Confederates from holding public office. Virginia and several other Southern states refused to sign, and were placed under military rule.

Military Reconstruction in Virginia lasted until a new state constitution, approved in 1870, gave African Americans the right to vote and allowed ex-Confederates to serve in office once again. Virginia was allowed to rejoin the Union it had left nine years earlier.

But a serious financial situation awaited Virginia's government. Before the war, the state invested heavily in building roads, canals, and railroads. The debt had risen to $45 million, with very little money to spare in the state treasury.

Members of the newly formed Conservative Party wanted to pay off the debt as quickly as possible. They passed the Funding Act in 1871, requiring the state to pay everything within thirty-four years. This move meant that money had to be taken away from the public school system and other state services.

A group known as the Readjusters felt that this payment schedule placed too heavy a burden on the state. Led by railroad magnate (and former Confederate general) William Mahone, the Readjusters formed a new political party.

Between 1879 and 1881, they won control of the General Assembly and the governorship and succeeded in reducing the debt considerably. They made sure schools had enough funding and outlawed the poll tax, a fee designed to prevent African Americans from voting.

The late 19th century saw a period

of economic growth in the Old Dominion. Railroad expansion linked the entire state. The Norfolk & Western Railroad brought the coal of southwestern Virginia to the port of Norfolk, where it could be shipped to other cities on the Atlantic Coast. The completion of the Chesapeake & Ohio Railroad in 1889 transformed the small town of Newport News into the home of one of the largest shipyards in the world.

Richmond boomed as a center of tobacco manufacturing while Danville developed a large textile industry. The town of Big Lick (later renamed Roanoke) grew from 400 people in 1881 to 25,000 by 1892 after becoming the junction of the Norfolk & Western and Pennsylvania railroads.

Farmers did not share the overall

This wood engraving, published in Harper's Weekly *on January 15, 1887, shows women rolling and packing cigarettes in a Richmond cigarette factory. Cigarette manufacturing became a very important industry in Richmond, and many women—black and white—went to work in the factories. The races were segregated and performed different tasks.*

prosperity. Low crop prices and high shipping costs led them to form the Farmers' Alliance in the 1880s. By 1890, this organization claimed 30,000 members and, in an attempt to regain political control from the railroad interests, formed the Virginia Populist Party in 1892. Populist candidates ran unsuccessfully in both the presidential and governor's race. In 1896, bowing to defeat, the party joined the higher-profile Democrats. Virginia remained a one-party state.

Virginia Enters a New Century

At the turn of the century, a constitutional convention met to rewrite the constitution of 1869. Many Virginia Democrats wanted to deny the vote to African Americans, in part because their loyalty to the Republican Party made it the state's strongest party.

Posters like Howard Chandler Christy's 1917 *I Want You For the Navy* were extremely effective in recruiting young men into the armed services. Virginians volunteered in large numbers and Norfolk led the nation in recruiting early in World War I.

The new constitution, adopted in 1902, brought back the poll tax. All voters were required to pay a $1.50 registration fee before becoming eligible to vote. A voter also had to register "in his own handwriting, without aid, suggestion, or memorandum, in the presence of registration officers."

Since many African Americans were poor and unable to read and write, the constitution effectively eliminated them (along with some poor whites) as a voting force. Between the 1901 and 1905 governor's elections, the African-American vote dropped by 88,000. In addition, the constitution legalized segregation, and over the next few decades, laws were passed that separated the races in schools and most public places.

Both economically and socially, Virginia changed rapidly in the first two decades of the 20th century. The Old Dominion began its long shift from a rural, farm-based economy to an urban, industrial-based one. Farms became smaller and more efficient, growing a wider variety of crops, and were not so dependent on tobacco. Agricultural prices improved as fewer people made a living as farmers.

World War I stimulated the economy and hastened migration to the cities. Newport News and Hampton Roads benefited from the naval shipyards and bases located there. Northern Virginia experienced its first spurt of growth as Washington expanded. During this time, many Virginians volunteered to serve in the Great War and nearly 1,200 gave their lives in that conflict. Even greater numbers died in the influenza epidemic following the war—11,641 in the Old Dominion alone.

In the early 1920s, Harry F. Byrd, a man who would dominate Virginia politics for more than forty-five years, began his political career as a state senator. He ran for governor in 1926 and was easily elected.

He spent four productive years in Richmond. Byrd's political thinking was based on the idea of "pay as you go." He did not believe in going into debt to finance public projects, so he paid for his extensive highway improvement program with a gasoline tax. He made state government more

After the war, the Virginia women's suffrage movement gathered momentum. Women made huge contributions to the war effort at home, and many felt they should have the right to vote. They won this right in 1920. The two women pictured here (top) are staffing a voter registration booth in Richmond shortly after the passage of the Nineteenth Amendment.

Harry F. Byrd, Sr., (1887–1966) (right) dominated Virginia's politics for forty years. As governor from 1926–30, he improved and expanded the state's highway system, reorganized state government, and ended his term with more than $4 million in the state treasury.

efficient and responsive to the people's demands.

Byrd encouraged business development and also created Shenandoah National Park. In order to build the park, 465 families had to give up their homes and were relocated by the government. President Franklin Roosevelt's Civilian Conservation Corps—a program set up during the Depression to allow young men the opportunity to earn money by improving the nation's parks, forests, and recreation areas—was instrumental in building the trails, bridges, and overlooks that still exist in the park today. In addition, the men planted trees, fought forest fires, and controlled soil erosion.

Byrd also enacted a law against lynching that effectively wiped out

The creation of Shenandoah National Park was authorized by Congress in 1926. Virginia then bought nearly 280 square miles of rugged, mountainous land in the Blue Ridge Mountains to establish the park. Although there were relatively few people living in the area at the time, 465 mountain families had to be relocated by the government.

this horrible and illegal practice. After his term as governor, he went on to become a U.S. senator where he continued to have an enormous effect on state politics until his death in 1966.

Thanks in part to Byrd's responsible financial policies, Virginia suffered less during the Depression than other states. On the eve of World War II, the state was poised to enter into a period of rapid economic growth followed by the most significant social changes since Reconstruction.

Wars at Home and Abroad

The United States' entry into World War II signaled the beginning of a defense build up of massive proportion. Virginia played a leading role in helping the country become, in Roosevelt's words, the "arsenal of democracy."

The war accelerated the growth of areas already affected by the military production of the First World War. The Hampton Roads area became a major center of naval shipbuilding and operation. The Norfolk Naval Air Base expanded, hiring thousands of workers, and the naval shipyard began building aircraft carriers and other warships for the war in the Atlantic Ocean. By 1943, the shipyard employed 43,000 people. The privately owned Newport News Shipbuilding and Dry Dock Company experienced similar growth, turning out ships around the clock.

Other parts of the state benefited from the war effort. Fort A. P. Hill, carved out of the farmland of Caroline County, became a major military base. Radford was home to the Hercules Powder Plant, a munitions factory that employed 20,000 people by the end of the war.

Northern Virginia, in particular, grew at a remarkable rate because of its closeness to Washington. The decision to build the Pentagon across the

This photograph shows the christening of the 23,547-ton aircraft carrier *Enterprise* on October 3, 1936, at the Newport News Shipbuilding and Dry Dock Company. The carrier saw plenty of action in World War II—it was damaged fifteen times in combat and destroyed seventy-one enemy ships and more than 900 planes.

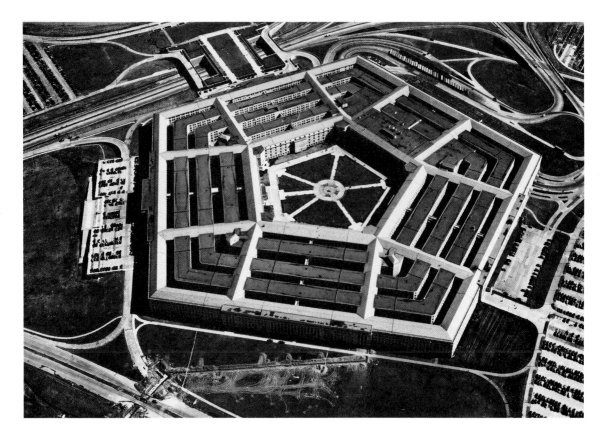

The Pentagon in Arlington was completed in January 1943. It is the largest office building in the world—with nearly 4 million square feet of floor space—and houses the Department of Defense and the headquarters of the army, navy, and air force.

By the late 1940s, the desegregation movement gained enough strength to attack some of the Jim Crow laws on buses and trains. In this 1946 photograph from the *Washington Star*, a man takes down a sign ordering African Americans to sit in the rear of a northern Virginia bus. It wasn't until after the mid-1950s, however, that widespread discrimination on public transportation began to end.

Potomac River in Arlington continued the capital city's expansion into the Virginia suburbs.

More than 300,000 Virginians served in the war, and almost 10,000 were killed in action. One of the most distinguished generals of the war, Army Chief of Staff George C. Marshall, author of the postwar Marshall Plan for rebuilding Europe, graduated from the Virginia Military Institute.

After the war, Virginia, like the rest of the country, was changed forever. There was no immediate slump in the economy and prosperity continued in the 1950s. African-American Virginians, however, did not share in the overall good times. When the issue of civil rights for blacks came to the forefront of national politics in the early 1950s, the turmoil in Virginia would last for more than a decade.

For the past fifty years, Virginia's Jim Crow laws had kept blacks and whites separate in public places. While the majority of white Virginians probably felt that the laws served the public good or that their race situation was not as bad as in some Deep South states, blacks certainly felt differently.

As in other Southern states, African Americans began moving away in large numbers—primarily to the District of Columbia. Segregation of the races was so deeply imbedded in day-to-day life that it seemed impossible to change.

On May 17, 1954, the U.S. Supreme Court's decision to end segregation in public schools set in motion the process of integration. This meant that African Americans would finally have access to the same educational opportunities as whites. In Virginia, as in the rest of the South, this change did not come easily.

Senator Byrd strongly opposed integration, as did many white Virginians. In 1957, Byrd's organization pushed through the legislation for massive resistance, which cut off all state funding for schools that accepted integration. In the fall of 1958, Governor Lindsay Almond shut down nine schools in Front Royal, Charlottesville, and Norfolk rather than integrate them.

Faced with actual closings, public opinion began to shift away from supporting massive resistance. When the federal district court in Norfolk and the Virginia State Supreme Court of Appeals both ruled against the policy, Governor Almond changed his position. Virginia's schools were reopened in 1959 and the long process of integration began peacefully. Only one county, Prince Edward, refused to integrate, and its schools were not reopened until 1964.

Massive resistance turned out to be the Byrd organization's downfall. Byrd and his party, despite many worthy achievements, failed to keep up with events or the changing nature of Virginia politics. After his death in 1966, the organization never regained its former influence.

The Changing Face of Virginia

The Old Dominion changed rapidly in the years following school desegregation. Virginia's Jim Crow laws, which had kept the races separated for so long, were gradually wiped off the books in an attempt to close an unpleasant chapter in the state's history.

There were also important voting changes on the federal and state levels. In 1964 and 1966, respectively, the poll tax was abolished in both federal and state elections. Now anyone of legal age could vote, regardless of how much money they had.

Also, in 1964, a Supreme Court ruling led the General Assembly to rework itself along a "one man, one vote" basis. This gave more voting power to urban areas and broadened Virginia's voting population.

The election of Democrat Mills E. Godwin, Jr., as governor in 1966 illustrated the final collapse of the Byrd organization. He abandoned Byrd's "pay-as-you-go" method of financing state services. While the old system was a good way to prevent spending more money than was available, it did not provide enough money for building schools, hospitals, and roads. As a result of Godwin's reforms, these essential services were greatly improved in Virginia.

In 1964, the Chesapeake Bay Bridge-Tunnel linking the Norfolk area with Virginia's Eastern Shore was completed. At seventeen miles long, it remains the longest bridge-tunnel in the world. Improved highways, interstates, and bridges made traveling easier for Virginia's population, which by 1970 was nearly 5 million people.

Much of the state remained rural, but the tide had shifted in favor of the city. The Washington suburbs reached to Fairfax County and into the counties of Loudon and Prince William. Northern Virginia could now be considered the southern endpoint of a great Eastern megacity that stretched all the way from Boston.

However, the Hampton Roads area, on the southern Virginia coast, was by now the largest urban area in the state. It still owed most of its growth to the U.S. Navy presence and the popularity of Virginia Beach with tourists.

Shifts in population and changes in society usually mean political change, and the Old Dominion has been no exception. In 1970, Virginians elected the first Republican governor since Reconstruction, Linwood Holton. He was followed by two consecutive Republicans before the Democrats regained the office in 1982. Virginia's days as a one-party state were over.

The Chesapeake Bay Bridge-Tunnel, a seventeen-mile-long highway across Chesapeake Bay, is made up of alternating steel bridges and tunnels. Each tunnel is built under a major shipping channel between artificial islands to allow vessels to pass.

New Challenges for the Old Dominion

In 1989, Virginia made national history when it elected L. Douglas Wilder, the country's first African-American governor. He served until 1993, when Republican George F. Allen defeated him in the governor's election.

Virginia's economy and population continued to grow during the 1980s and early 1990s. Yet development has occurred mainly in what has come to be called the state's "golden crescent." This area, connected by a grid of interstate highways, stretches from northern Virginia to Richmond and on to Hampton Roads.

Northern Virginia has in recent years attracted high-tech firms and is home to the state's Center for Innovative Technology, whose president is former governor Holton.

Richmond today is a leading city in the "New South." With the cigarette and consumer goods corporation Philip Morris USA headquartered there (employing more than 11,000 people), Richmond can claim thirteen of the country's largest corporations, including the paper company James River and Reynolds Metals, manufacuers of aluminum foil.

This view of downtown Richmond's skyline shows the heart of the Old Dominion's capital. The city is a vibrant mixture of old and new Virginia, with museums, monuments, and historic districts existing side by side with Fortune 500 companies, fine restaurants, and lovely parks.

The Hampton Roads area is still an important naval area and international shipping center. The Norfolk Naval base, the largest in the world, boasts two four-star admirals: one is the commander-in-chief of NATO's Atlantic operations, and the other is the commander-in-chief of the U.S. Atlantic fleet.

The naval shipyard in nearby Portsmouth was built in 1767 and it was there that the first battleship (the USS Texas in 1892) and aircraft carrier (the USS Langley in 1922) were built. It recently survived a round of base closings, but its future is still uncertain.

The Newport News Shipbuilding and Dry Dock Company is the state's largest private employer, with almost 30,000 employees. Nearly 64 million tons of import-export cargo goes through the Virginia Port Authority in Norfolk each year, making it the fastest-growing port in the country.

Growth, in fact, has not come without problems in Virginia. To a great extent, the state's rural regions have not shared in northeastern Virginia's prosperity. Southern Virginia faces the collapse of its 300-year-old tobacco economy due to government attempts to regulate the tobacco industry. The closing of several coal mines in southwestern Virginia has brought much economic hardship to area residents.

With growth has come pollution. The most pressing problem for Virginia is the collapse of the once rich Chesapeake Bay fishery. Until recently, the bay was one of the country's most bountiful sources of oysters, crabs, flounder, and rockfish. Pollution from agriculture and industry and increased bayside development has caused the harvest to decline dramatically. Fortunately, the problem was recognized early and state and private organizations are working hard to save the bay.

Tourism may provide some economic relief. Virginia is rich in easily accessible historical sites—Colonial Williamsburg, Monticello, Mount Vernon—and the many Civil War battlefields are popular tourist attractions.

No issue in recent years has divided the state more than the Walt Disney Company's 1993 announcement that it intended to build a historical theme park near several Civil War historic battlefields in northern Virginia. Many people welcomed the park because they felt it would provide thousands of jobs and would increase tourism. But others thought that the battlefields should be preserved as a reminder of our country's history.

In the summer of 1994, Disney decided not to build the park in that location. The controversy showed that Virginians care deeply about their history. It also points out the increasingly difficult path ahead for Virginia as its urban areas expand and its countryside shrinks. The question remains whether the Old Dominion can retain its historical identity while providing a future for its residents.

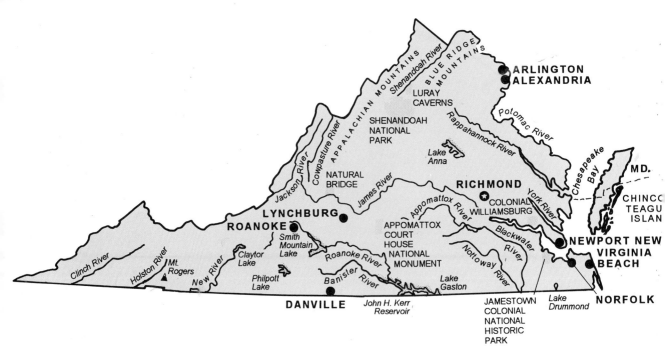

Land Area:
39,578 square miles, of which 1,063 are inland water. Ranks 36th in size.

Major rivers:
The James; the Potomac; the Rappahannock; the Appomattox; the York; the Roanoke; the Shenandoah; the New; the Holston; the Clinch; the Blackwater; the Nottoway; the Banister; the Jackson; the Cowpasture.

Highest Point:
Mt. Rogers, 5,729 ft.

Major Bodies of Water:
Chesapeake Bay; Lake Drummond; Lake Anna; Smith Mountain Lake; John H. Kerr Reservoir; Lake Gaston; Philpott Lake; Claytor Lake.

Climate:
Average January temperature: 36°F
Average July temperature: 75°F

Population: 6,377,141 (1992)
Rank: 12th
    1900: 1,854,184
    1790: 691,737

Population of major cities (1990):

Virginia Beach	393,069
Norfolk	261,229
Richmond	203,056
Arlington	170,936
Newport News	170,045
Alexandria	111,183
Roanoke	96,397
Lynchburg	66,049

Ethnic breakdown by percentage (1990):

White	76.0%
African American	18.6%
Hispanic	2.6%
Asian	2.5%
Native American	0.2%

Economy:
    Government services; agriculture; manufacturing (tobacco products, shipbuilding, electronic equipment, processed foods, textiles, light machinery); mining; fishing; and tourism.

State government:
    Legislature: The 40-member Senate and 100-member House of Delegates make up the General Assembly. Senators serve terms of 4 years, delegates serve 2 years.
    Governor: The governor, elected for a 4-year term, heads the executive branch. He may not succeed himself in office.
    Courts: The state supreme court consists of 7 judges elected by the General Assembly for 12-year terms. There are circuit courts for counties and towns. The General Assembly elects circuit court judges for 8 years.
State capital: Richmond

State Flag

A deep blue field with a circular white center containing the state coat of arms; a white silk fringe on the outer edge. Virginia adopted this design for the flag in 1931.

State Seal

The seal for Virginia bears the state coat of arms: the Goddess of Virtue resting on her spear. Under her foot is the defeated body of Tyranny. At the top is the state name and below the state motto.

State Motto

Sic Temper Tyrannis, which means "Thus Always to Tyrants." The motto dates to the time of the American Revolution.

State Nickname

Virginia's most common nickname is "The Old Dominion," because it was England's oldest colony in America. Other nicknames include, the "Cavalier State," the "Mother of Presidents," and the "Mother of States."

Places

Appomattox Court House National Monument, Appomattox

Arlington National Cemetery, Arlington

Ashlawn-Highland, Charlottesville

Barter Theatre, Abingdon

Booker T. Washington National Monument, Roanoke

Busch Gardens, Williamsburg

Chincoteague Island, Chincoteague

Christ Church, Alexandria

Cumberland Gap National Historic Park, Ewing

Edgar Allen Poe Museum, Richmond

Emancipation Oak, Hampton

First Landing Cross, Virginia Beach

Fort Monroe, Hampton

Fredericksburg and Spotsylvania National Military Park, Fredericksburg

Gadsby's Tavern, Alexandria

George C. Marshall Museum, Lexington

George Washington Birthplace, Colonial Beach

Governor's Palace, Williamsburg

Great Falls Park, Great Falls

Jamestown Colonial National Historic Park, Williamsburg

Lee Chapel, Lexington

Manassas National Battlefield Park, Manassas

to See

Monticello,
Charlottesville

Mount Vernon,
Mount Vernon

Museum of
Frontier Culture,
Staunton

Museum of the
Confederacy,
Richmond

Naval Shipyard
Museum,
Portsmouth

New Market
Battlefield,
New Market

Norfolk Botanical
Garden, Norfolk

Norfolk Naval Base,
Norfolk

Old Cape Henry
Lighthouse,
Virginia Beach

Pentagon, Arlington

Poplar Forest,
Lynchburg

Shenandoah
National Park,
Front Royal

Southwest Virginia
Museum,
Big Stone Gap

Stratford Hall,
Colonial Beach

The Homestead,
Hot Springs

Valentine Museum,
Richmond

Virginia Air and
Space Center,
Hampton

Virginia Marine
Science Museum,
Virginia Beach

Virginia Museum
of Fine Arts,
Richmond

Wolf Trap Center
for the Performing
Arts, Vienna

Yorktown Victory
Center,
Yorktown

State Flower

Virginia's state flower is the flower of the American dogwood tree. It is white to greenish-yellow and blooms in the spring.

State Bird

Virginia's state bird is the cardinal, recognizable by bright red feathers (in the male), and loud, flutelike whistles. Cardinals primarily eat grain and fruit.

State Tree

The American dogwood is the official state tree of Virginia. Chosen in 1918, the dogwood is a small tree found throughout the East and Midwest. It has scaly bark and white flowers with scarlet fruit.

Virginia History

9500 b.c. Earliest evidence of native peoples in Virginia

1585 English settlers reach Roanoke Island

1591 Roanoke Colony found with no survivors

1607 Jamestown, the first permanent English settlement in the New World, is founded

1619 First blacks arrive in colony as indentured servants

1624 Virginia becomes a royal colony

1661 Slavery is legalized

1676 Bacon leads rebellion against Governor Berkeley

1699 Capital moves from Jamestown to Williamsburg

1716 Governor Spotswood leads expedition over the Blue Ridge Mountains

1765 The General Assembly passes the Stamp Act Resolves

1774 Virginia Convention calls for first Continental Congress

1776 Virginia becomes independent, Patrick Henry is first governor

1780 Capital moved to Richmond

1781 Cornwallis surrenders at Yorktown

1788 Virginia ratifies the U.S. Constitution and becomes tenth state

1789 George Washington becomes first president of the United States

American

1492 Christopher Columbus reaches the New World

1607 Jamestown (Virginia) founded by English colonists

1620 *Mayflower* arrives at Plymouth (Massachusetts)

1754-63 French and Indian War

1765 Parliament passes Stamp Act

1775-83 Revolutionary War

1776 Signing of the Declaration of Independence

1788-90 First congressional elections

1791 Bill of Rights added to U.S. Constitution

1803 Louisiana Purchase

1812-14 War of 1812

1820 Missouri Compromise

1836 Battle of the Alamo, Texas

1846-48 Mexican-American War

1849 California Gold Rush

1860 South Carolina secedes from Union

1861-65 Civil War

1862 Lincoln signs Homestead Act

1863 Emancipation Proclamation

1865 President Lincoln assassinated (April 14)

1865-77 Reconstruction in the South

1866 Civil Rights bill passed

1881 President James Garfield shot (July 2)

History

1896 First Ford automobile is made

1898–99 Spanish-American War

1901 President William McKinley is shot (Sept. 6)

1917 U.S. enters World War I

1922 Nineteenth Amendment passed, giving women the vote

1929 U.S. stock market crash; Great Depression begins

1933 Franklin D. Roosevelt becomes president; begins New Deal

1941 Japanese attack Pearl Harbor (Dec. 7); U.S. enters World War II

1945 U.S. drops atomic bomb on Hiroshima and Nagasaki; Japan surrenders, ending World War II

1963 President Kennedy assassinated (November 22)

1964 Civil Rights Act passed

1965–73 Vietnam War

1968 Martin Luther King, Jr., shot in Memphis (April 4)

1974 President Richard Nixon resigns because of Watergate scandal

1979–81 Hostage crisis in Iran: 52 Americans held captive for 444 days

1989 End of U.S.-Soviet cold war

1991 Gulf War

1993 U.S. signs North American Free Trade Agreement with Canada and Mexico

Virginia History

1801 Thomas Jefferson becomes third president

1816 Western Virginians demand equal representation

1831 Nat Turner leads a slave revolt, leading to stricter laws on slavery

1851 A new state constitution allows all white males to vote

1859 John Brown leads raid at Harpers Ferry

1861 Virginia secedes from the Union and Richmond becomes the Confederate capital; Civil War begins

1865 Lee surrenders to Grant at Appomattox

1870 Virginia is readmitted to the Union

1900 State legislature passes "Jim Crow" laws, implementing segregation

1902 New laws restrict voting by a poll tax and literacy requirements

1913 Woodrow Wilson becomes the twenty-eighth U.S. president

1954 U.S. Supreme Court ruling ends segregation in the South

1964 U.S. Supreme Court orders all public schools desegregated

1972 Hurricane Agnes devastates region

1989 Democrat L. Douglas Wilder is first African American elected governor in U.S. history

Wahunsunacock (c. 1547–1618) An Indian chief of the Powhatan tribe, Wahunsunacock (also known as Powhatan) ruled over thirty-two other lesser chiefs in 150 villages at the time of the English arrival.

Pocahontas (1595–1617) The daughter of Powhatan, Pocahontas was famous for saving the life of John Smith. She later married English settler John Rolfe.

George Washington (1732– 99) The first president of the United States, Washington was a surveyor in his youth. He was a military leader in the French and Indian War and in the Revolutionary War. He is known as "The Father of His Country."

Patrick Henry (1736–99) With his famous "Give me liberty or give me death" speech, Henry marked himself as one of the leaders of the American Revolution. He served twice as governor of Virginia.

Thomas Jefferson (1743– 1826) The third president of the United States, Jefferson was born in Albemarle County. He drafted the Declaration of Independence and served as secretary of state under Washington. After his retirement, he founded the University of Virginia.

James Madison (1751–1836) Madison was the fourth president of the United States. Earlier, he had played a key role in drafting the Constitution.

John Marshall (1755–92) The fourth chief justice of the U.S. Supreme Court, Marshall helped raise the Supreme Court's prestige and established many basic ideas for interpreting the Constitution.

Henry Lee (1756–1818) Lee was a Revolutionary War hero present at the signing of the Declaration of Independence. He later became a governor of Virginia and served as a congressman. He was the father of Robert E. Lee.

James Monroe (1758–1831) Fifth president of the United States, Monroe attended William and Mary College and studied law under Thomas Jefferson.

Nat Turner (1800–31) A slave who led one of the few slave rebellions in U.S. history, Turner and his followers killed sixty people in Southampton County before he was caught and hanged.

Cyrus McCormick (1809–1884) McCormick was an inventor born in Rockbridge County who invented the reaper, a machine that revolutionized farming.

Robert E. Lee (1807–70) A brilliant general of the Confederate Army in the Civil War, Lee managed to win many victories despite facing overwhelming odds.

Edgar Allan Poe (1809–49) Raised in Richmond, Poe was a poet, critic, and short story writer. He is the author of horror stories like *The Fall of*

Edgar Allen Poe

the House of Usher and poems such as *The Raven*.

Thomas J. "Stonewall" Jackson (1824–63) Considered one of the most outstanding generals in military history, Jackson fought for the Confederacy.

Walter Reed (1851–1902) A U.S. Army surgeon born in Belroi, Reed proved that yellow fever was carried by mosquitos.

Booker T. Washington (1856–1915) Born a slave near Roanoke, Washington became a noted educator and founded Tuskegee Institute in Alabama in 1881.

Maggie Walker (1867–1934) The child of a former slave, Walker became a successful businesswoman and the first female bank president in the United States.

Bill "Bojangles" Robinson (1878–1949) A well-known and talented dancer, this Richmond native starred in many films in the 1930s.

Harry Flood Byrd, Sr. (1887–1966) One of Virginia's foremost politicians, Byrd served as governor from 1926–30 and as U.S. senator from 1933–65.

Richard E. Byrd (1888–1957) A Winchester native, Byrd became the first person to fly over the North and South poles.

Sam Snead (b. 1912) A professional golfer born near Hot Springs, Snead won three PGA titles, three Masters, and one British Open during his career.

Ella Fitzgerald (b. 1918) Fitzgerald, called the First Lady of Song, was an internationally-known jazz singer. Her first hit was "A-Tisket A-Tasket" in 1938.

Maggie Walker

William Styron (b. 1924) Born in Newport News, Styron is one of the most acclaimed novelists living today. Several of his books have been set in Virginia, most notably *The Confessions of Nat Turner*. He won the Pulitzer prize for *Sophie's Choice*.

George C. Scott (b. 1927) Born in the small town of Wise, Scott is an acclaimed actor. He won an Academy Award in 1970 for the title role in the movie *Patton*.

L. Douglas Wilder (b. 1931) Born in Richmond, Wilder had a long political career in state government before being elected the first African-American governor in the nation in 1989.

Tom Wolfe (b. 1931) A respected journalist and writer, Wolfe is a Richmond native. He is best known for *The Bonfire of the Vanities*.

Patsy Cline (1932–63) Born in Winchester, Cline's fame as a country music singer was cut short in a tragic plane crash. She had many hits, including "Sweet Dreams" and "Crazy."

Arthur Ashe (1943–93) A Richmond native, Ashe became the first African American to win the Wimbledon men's singles championship in 1975.

Pictures in this volume:

Colonial National Historical Park: 17

Dover: 2

Gunston Hall: 35

Library of Congress: 7, 9, 10, 12, 13, 14 (top), 14 (bottom), 15, 16, 19, 20, 21, 23, 24, 26, 27, 29, 30, 31, 32, 33, 34, 36, 37, 38-39, 40, 43, 45 (bottom), 48 (top), 60

The Library of Virginia: 42, 47

National Archives: 41, 44

National Park Service: 46, 61

Dennis M. Nicoll: 51

Valentine Museum, Richmond, Virginia: 45 (top)

Virginia Division of Tourism: 2, 52

Copyright *Washington Post*, reprinted by permission of the D.C. Public Library: 48 (bottom)

About the author:

William Cocke lives in Lexington, Virginia. He is a contributing editor at the alumni magazine at Washington and Lee University, where he also writes for the news office. An avid outdoorsman, Mr. Cocke has contributed articles to local newspapers and magazines, primarily on natural history.

Suggested Reading:

Egloff, Keith and Woodward, Deborah, *First People: The Early Indians of Virginia*, Richmond: Virginia Department of Historic Resources, 1992

Fishwick, Marshall W., *Jamestown: First English Colony*, New York: American Heritage Publishing Co., 1965

Fradin, Dennis B., *Virginia*, Chicago: Childrens Press, 1992

McNair, Sylvia, *Virginia*, Chicago: Children's Press, 1989

Sirvaitis, Karen, *Virginia*, Minneapolis: Lerner Publishing Co., 1991

Thane, Elswyth, *The Virginia Colony*, New York: Cromwell-Collier Press, 1969

For more information contact:

Virginia Division of Tourism
1021 East Cary Street, Tower II
Richmond, Virginia 23219
Tel. (804) 786-2051

The Library of Virginia
11th Street at Capitol Square
Richmond, Virginia 23219-3491
Tel. (804) 786-2332

INDEX

Page numbers in *italics* indicate illustrations